Shakespeare's Birthday

Also by Peter Levi

POETRY
Collected Poems 1955-1975   *1976*
Five Ages   *1978*
Private Ground   *1981*
The Echoing Green   *1983*

TRANSLATIONS
Yevtushenko: Selected Poems   *1962*
Pausanias: Guide to Greece   *1971*
The Psalms   *1976*
Pavlopoulos: The Cellar   *1977*
Marko the Prince *(with Anne Pennington)*   *1983*

FICTION
The Head in the Soup   *1979*
Grave Witness   *1985*

PROSE
The Light Garden of the Angel King   *1973*
The English Bible   *1974*
The Noise Made by Poems   *1977*
The Hill of Kronos   *1980*
Atlas of the Greek World   *1980*
The Flutes of Autumn   *1983*
The Lamentation of the Dead   *1984*
A History of Greek Literature   *1985*

Peter Levi

Shakespeare's Birthday

Anvil Press Poetry

Published in 1985
by Anvil Press Poetry Ltd
69 King George Street London SE10 8PX

ISBN 0 85646 142 3

Photoset in Ehrhardt
by Bryan Williamson
Printed in England
by the Arc & Throstle Press
Todmorden, Lancs

This book is published
with financial assistance from
The Arts Council of Great Britain

Contents

for Deirdre

Note

These three lamentations of the dead are printed in the order in which they were written. They are in the same form as others I have already published, but there are also differences that express personality. I do not think I will ever write in this form again, because its variations are not infinite, although they have been sufficient for these poems. Caryl Brahms was my favourite cousin; she was Jewish, and much older than I was. Charles Haldeman was an American of my own age; he was a poet and a novelist. He lived in Greece, and we met there in 1963 through Nikos Gatsos. Charles died very suddenly of an unattended infection, by bleeding to death. Alasdair Clayre was a philosopher, a poet, a song-writer, and in the end (like Charles) a film-maker, who had been my friend since we were at Oxford together in the fifties. He died by suicide in a moment of severe depression. Since they were all writers, these poems refer sometimes to their own writings, as well as to other things they liked or would have liked. The quotations in italics are from Nikos Gatsos, Peter Huchel (twice), a Chinese poem translated by Alasdair, Malory, a medieval Latin song, and Heine.

P.L.

For Charles Haldeman

died 19 January 1983

FOR CHARLES HALDEMAN

I

The transmutations of the sea:
shifting glitter, shadow and splash,
body of cold and lucid fire
speaking through foam as white as ash:

unwritten poem in the waves
that only heave and fall and fume,
and hardly whisper in their sleep
the poetry that they consume.

A small hill like a spiky breast
summons the sailor from the sea,
as if the bell had clarified
and frozen to eternity.

II

And so the wisest love what is living
and some of the most living love the wise:
prophet and poet will endure to die,
his shutters warp and rattle in the sun
and the sun wears away colours from wood,
he woos the wild cat out of the weeds
that nested in the rubble and thistles,
he hears the thrush sing on the dolphin-bones,
and will survey the sober waves on fire
at the late rising of the winter sun.
There was one café on the empty quay,
it could consume poetry in handfuls
never distracted from the stone quayside.
High overhead under the blazing sun
a snowy mountain rippled like a flag.
In the morning wrote letters for the whores
to their true loves serving in Sicily,
with eyes of blue, far clearer than the sea.

III

South Carolina squirrels in the pines
chattered and ran in nineteen thirty-one,
dancing among the shadows of their tails;
pine-cones that ripen in the hot season
lay gasping in the dusty forest rides,
squirrels scattered and hid in the blue pines.
Pure Gaelic blood and German forest blood:
our generation is rooted in war,
there are no squirrels in the knotted pines.
Lover of Jews and gipsy poetry,
saw the old people, I never saw mine.
Then the U.S. navy: enlisted man
in sea-roads that the dolphins cleared of dead;
the sea swung and death picked the metal bare,
dolphins floated the dead to Florida
whose service is to clean the streaming sea.
Not in your time at sea, not in my time.
Charles, we were boys when War almighty reigned
and armaments and fleets sank in the sea
with fire and oil and guns and crated goods
and drowning cries and souls of slaughtered men.
As we measure it, you died young my friend,
yet we were old, we had lived to be old.

IV

Waves like blue tigers fawn on island rocks
lashing against the rock with tails of foam.
In the mountains in shelter irt the sun
in shade from light, in snowy-smelling air
under the plane-tree by the water-spring
a walnut cracking in an old man's hand.
The sun's harsh colours in the snow and sky
lit up the shadow colour of the rock
and the rock-weeds, the lilies in the grass;
how freshly the skin-tone crept on the fruit
that ripened through three seasons of the year.
Spring was a smell of gunsmoke in the air,
gunshots re-echoed from the mountainside,
echoed, echoed, echoed, echoed and died.
Honey of those mountains, fresh-gathered tea,
the dewy thistles, shepherds, the wild goats
cropping arbutus on the dry mountain:
pure paradise stirring no memory:
eternal heavens withered overhead
and wept comets of whiteness and blood-red.
Crete was a postcard, bloodstained and smokestained.
Who had endured to die their death bleeding.
A man creates his death like a poem
whom women will lament in true poems.

Still in old caverns in the high mountains
where God newborn was suckled by a goat
a man becomes a legend in ruins,
the circling mountains and cold-blooded sea
speak in raw lightning flashes to all men
and childish God, fated in innocence
to suffer life and to live out his life
on mountains of luxurious freedom.
Stone, light, and black sea. Nothing else at all.
Heaven had melted in the hermit's eye,
white villages, and the dark, molten trees;
moonlight had washed the innocent island
and your life melted in the wish to live.
The golden sun that lives in its own west
carries away the mountains to their rest.

V

Let them go naked into black water
with wine and leaves and kisses in their mouth.
A little grain kept for the festival,
wine for remembrance, water for the dust.
The viper streaking through the barleyfield
whose eyes the lightning threshes in their pride
endures a poetry that is not said.
So when the sun climbs into her window,
and strokes her in her gold and in her snow
and warms her through, her first word is to you.
At other times under the lamp at night
while their lover is dancing by lamplight
the trees in leaf are crowding through the dark,
ruins of cuckoo-calls fade in the trees,
you have walked away homewards and have left
the quayside empty under the street-lights.
In Athens once under the castle wall
night-wind plucked away paper from our hands,
no moisture and no coolness in the wind,
but as if three poets sat in a cave
of airy darkness and the chaff of stars,
and smells of watered jasmine and of dust.
Played out our hands in poems line by line,
proceeding consequence by consequence,

until the wind that finishes seasons
had blown the dark to tatters and the stars.
You were not fated by the fall of lines
and will not come as the dead do to drink
wine spilt for memory, water for dust:
in foliage of the vineyard you sleep,
in the fresh tendrils of the stringy vine
and wooden juices of the stony vine.
Abandoning poem after poem,
the clearest and blackest of watersprings,
mountain ash, mountain plane, shade cyclamen
shadowed a deeper colour than the sun,
the cold colours of dawn and of dewfall,
all that dies in unwritten poetry.
Now the shadows have toppled from the crest
and sprawl for ever down the mountainside,
we must breathe the dark liquid of our lives.
It is as if you never had been old,
as if oak trees ran honey unrefined:
it is as if blue days groaned in their grave,
or once in the enchanted summer wind
dark lightning flashed and played around your head,
all poetry unwritten and most pure
voice of eros, whisper of thanatos.
It is as if that night never ended,
it is as if you never had been born.

VI

How swiftly day breaks and how silently
darkness goes sliding down under the sea.
In caverns of the sea there is no death
no roaring pebbles and no barren breath,
only half-light, the green and silver stain,
and the sea groaning again and again.
In poems we have breathed away our breath,
and the last poem of the soul is death;
it is a withering when the soul dies,
the barren wave rejoices, the bird flies.
Slowly, slowly, we breathed our souls away,
then your blood ran as quickly as the day.
The bravest and the straightest and the best
who lose the most go soonest to their rest.
How swiftly the night falls, how silently
island and mountain sink into the sea.

For Caryl Brahms

died 5 December 1982

FOR CARYL BRAHMS

I

Victorian stone children in the trees,
tall under streetlights that increase the dark:
they dream of taxis and of carriages
and of the sun sinking above the park.

High in the flats your window opened out
on a small balcony like a stone shelf
to catch at weather and the distant shout
of the last echoes crying Know thyself.

The trees are dying with no noise at all
while the fresh leaf shivers in the fresh light,
leaf by leaf they will turn colour and fall.
The only monument we have is night.

II

My dearest, when your childhood had become
a ballet like a transformation scene,
and painful love glowed slowly in the air
never consumed, what you remembered was
dark thousand-petalled roses of that time
gathered in thunderstorms of garden scent,
the London thrush heaving his speckled breast,
cigarette smoke like phrases in Chekhov.
The French hill-garden, meagre lemon trees
above the stony dark and sparkling sea.
Poem after poem dissolved away.
Your mother's dresses treasured secretly
because you never could be beautiful,
and a passion for out of date postcards:
heaven opened in them in 1910,
on multicoloured swans that dying sang.
Then the rough wind, the sea's life-giving breath,
and victorious barrenness of the tide.

III

It is the Sabbath now, God has rested,
white snow-showers of stars whirl overhead,
straw-coloured whisps of fire to light the dead
as if time were a clockwork running down,
or the soul ran backward to its own place,
to where a generation hung like breath
among the apple-trees; it was Sabbath.
Will they be happy in two hundred years,
not as we live now, quiet Croydon roads
with bushes, grass and flowers out of hand,
whose hope was visionary in autumn
when the soul cries to her pure origin?
Tall houses, dark nourishment of the soul,
where the piano chimed a thousand hours
expressing hungers blinder than the grave,
and longer than the artifice of life.
Wine pouring into motionless cut glass,
beside bread under velvet and gold thread
with Hebrew lettering white on blood red.
It is the Sabbath now, God has rested.
Cousin, it is time now to light the lamp,
the tide that has carried so many dead
streams away down the bare sand of your life.

IV

When it is midday, and when the white fire
of poetry dances above the urns
remember them, my child, they have planted
their conversations in the earth like trees.
How that light foliage unprotected
comes crashing to the ground.
I am tied up with London of those years,
and the whole sky solemn and rose-coloured,
the firemen's bells and sirens and alarms,
when in one moment all houses grew pale
and groaned and blushed and crumbled to ruins.
Canyons of brown brick with their walls on fire,
and the high hoses weakly fountaining
over a wilderness of mad shadow:
your night-times and your wartime in the street,
the dusky fires swarming around your head
and iron clanging tears of molten bells
silted in the dark river of your soul,
when eastern sun, blood-cloud and thunder-cloud
mingled above Saint Paul's and his high dome,
and the dark angel brooding in the sun
wept at last and in pity turned away.
Cold red fire-weed and cat-infested stones.
Germany is dark. Germany is cold.

Therefore when I survey the wondrous cross
I am back in your lightless cobbled streets
that ran once on the south bank of the Thames,
that silence as the great dome rises there,
dreamed in the moons of summer by Shakespeare.
The rain has laid the dust on the plane trees
north of the river, that complaining wood
rustles from tree to tree, till the oldest
extend their heavy branches in the squares
in promises of lightest summer sleep.
Sleep dearest. It is time to sleep now.
Dawn has breasted Thames water like a swan,
she is drifting upstream with the new tide.
The sun is up, soon the milk will arrive,
the street is safe, the city is alive.

V

I will stand at the altar of my God
who will be praised in the name of the dead,
and blessed in a wilderness of voices.
All Israel is in the world to come,
as it was said, My people shall be just,
they shall inherit that land for ever,
branch of my planting, work of my own hand.
How bitter lilies smell in the late year,
where our old tea table has scarred the grass,
white swarms of jasmine climb the wall like bees,
and the tobacco flowers smell at night.
We did not travel through the leafless wood,
we have not seen the edges of mountains
crested with snow, six inches in the sky.
The grape rots on the wall of the greenhouse,
and will it ripen in the world to come?
We have sat warm by the fires of the wise,
but the coal glowed too bright and we were burnt:
and their bite is the bite of the fox,
and they sting with the sting of scorpions,
they hiss as a snake hisses, words of fire.
And now the darkening tree drenches the sun,
cool early summer of the world to come;
shall we have visions cousin in the grave?

Forget what this world was, what it shall be?
I praise my God in your name and in mine,
Sabbath comes and my tongue is withering
and will wither before the world to come.
Blessed art thou King of the universe
creator of the small fruits of the vine.
May we attain the festivals of years,
by God's mercy chanting praises to God.
Our life has been consumed among wonders,
dreamlike before the Sabbath rest of God
done drowsing in the twilight of that day,
and we have passed into the sleep of God.
The red and blue and grey and snow-white glass
that glimmered while your dinner-candles burned
and holy angel gilded on the wall
are gone now and the curtains have fallen,
one complete darkness has extinguished them.
My love is ghostly. I will praise my God.
And where the small car trundled up the lanes
below the pathless ocean of the downs,
while the pale cowslip deepened in the sun,
the spreading thyme and breathless violet
and your green peace in every corner sang,
they have sailed out of sight and are silent.
Your hours of time have melted from the clock
and the blue marbling of the moon's white sphere.

VI

Now the dry season droning through your head
and the unbodied spirits of the dead
cry out to Venus, where her mild planet
smoulders among the clinkers of sunset.
Now in black shadow while the moon is bright
long silver-throated music chants all night,
the nightingale only nightwalkers see,
loud bird of love and painful purity.
He has chanted for you in green branches
in secret muttering river-valleys.
The towers of his leaves are sad and high,
they will paint a fresh colour on the sky:
but we shall not be in the meadow then,
the breath of our words will be forgotten,
these woods and birdsong have buried our day.
What we acted was real. It was no play.

For Alasdair Clayre

died 10 January 1984

FOR ALASDAIR CLAYRE

I

Drowned in honeys of immortality
a city like a colony of swans
just woken from four hundred years of sleep
to wash away her soot from the white stones:

old scrawny heronry in the elm grove
brooding through may and rain and into june,
while the dark river shamed us with passion
as if the sky had painted the light green.

Soot-streaked and butter-coloured, barren stones
that breathed in harmony with heavy trees
lie gasping now and choked in traffic fumes,
and the old grove has died of elm disease.

II

That whiff of time expended like a breath
has left a memory as pure as ash:
we were overshadowed by illusions,
real muses were singing in Latin,
all your life was one long, musical breath,
architecture, fresh mazes of the soul
and the grave movement of philosophy,
libraries breaking open in green leaf.
You breathed your soul out heavy as a breath,
line after line, poem after poem,
imperfect, our music is imperfect.
It has the warmth and the small scale of life,
is in love with love as the soul is not.
Our life was like a ballroom in a tent
under obscurest circles of starlight,
a garden and the breath of cold all night:
then morning broke on London by daylight.
Another sun has climbed out of his east.

III

Socrates lost in God
the one loving the One:
all night and day he stood
frost-footed in the sun.
Clouds of Socratic leaf
are withered from that tree,
echoing songs of life
and immortality.
After philosophy when nothing lived
we foundered in philosophy of love:
drumbeat of spirit and the soul's retreat,
passion of the wild swan and his wingbeat
but tone deaf to the small music of love.
And rose arose the idle, quiet sun
who might unfreeze the cold blood of the sea,
then penetrate the snow, melt the snowbird,
ruffle long feathers of the snowy bird.
Because iron is truth, and the bronze bell
tolls away time with his true-telling tongue.
And it might be the music of the spheres
and the God who enraptured Socrates
spoke in the chiming of a German clock
like painted soldiers marching to music.

IV

Love is a nowhere country, who builds it?
It is where we should hide and be and build.
The lover unloved is the working class
and more complaining is the more unloved,
starving to death in nineteen forty-four.
The alcohol of folksong is no cure.
The universe of Newton and of Wren
drowned out the moon in Milton's poetry,
light stains the edges of night's handkerchief,
and you sleep on the dry leaf in the woods,
Alasdair, as children in stories sleep:
dark violets and cold white violets
open their face round the uncropped meadows,
the daffodil his cold and modest mouth,
without comfort or dewfall of the moon.
Because Utopia was our true place,
the chiming of the chisel and the pen.
It is in the condition of mankind:
work is not comedy but tragedy:
as no one else travelled so far to find.
The soul is in nature, in your nature
heaved and tumbled as cloud heaves at the sea;
nothing in life is boring but *grandeur*
or hangs so heavy in the eye of man.

Utopia: the country of a dream:
a mist of bluebells in the oak forest,
a trance of truth where we gazed on and on,
woke to the scratching of a willow twig,
the Chinese mountains, sharp decline of days
leaf by leaf shaken down and the few fruit,
loud voice of water in the mist and stone:
hills to the south a long way away:
it is sunset
the air over the mountains is beautiful;
birds are flying in flocks back to their nests,
this tastes real,
I would like to talk about it, there are no words.
William Morris is weaving your shroud,
in purest heaven you lie down to sleep
where love and reason are the evening stars.

V

The early bees are in the pear blossom;
they are droning away Shakespeare's birthday,
who lies under the flagstones of his church
or stares or drowses on the shadowed wall
in painted plaster, bones and earth, among
a labyrinth of rivers and meadows.
The pleated shroud and the old coffin wood
have crumbled in decaying dust with him,
who is the king in kingdoms underground.
Immortal spirit always withering
as the sun's fire ruins and ripens all,
touching the leaf and harvest with his fire:
rough blushing pear, crabshell and crust of stone.
Whose ghost has withered like smoke and is gone.
For love that time was not as love is now,
it is a twilight darker than a grape,
it is the wasting of a candle-flame,
not heaven's fire or spirit dropping down
which was the hermit and the saint of love.
You have drowned in that fire as I do now,
like those spirits the visionary saw
that danced in fire and dressed themselves in flame
singing in their motion like silver stars
among the coolest fires of purgatory.

Et philomena ceteris conqueritur
quod illis ignis aetheris adimitur.
The nightingale lamenting heaven's fire.
It is winter and the day's fire is out.
Now the machinery of time shivers
and sunset and daybreak have broken down.
The pale sky hangs in thin, exhausted trees:
no more scene-shifting, only a bare stage,
disease of mind, the last day of your life.
Pale sun like a bad angel perching on
his creaking hills of cloud recalls that day
when Milton's Lucifer whom Christ saw fall
sat like a bat upon the dome of Paul's.
Slow morning of storm-rain and of storm-wind,
it darkened, you were terribly torn off.
Our kitchen radio played that old song
I heard you sing for me when we were young,
Ich grolle nicht, while our small river ran
darkly in shadow of the wooden bridge.
If you could sleep. If you could only sleep.
Now that the time has come when you will sleep
and mildly dream a thinly painted sky,
sleep lightly, dream that you break out of sleep
into a morning drenched in light, and wild
cries of the birds in unfamiliar skies,
though they must freeze and weep when summer dies.

VI

The last pure light is streaming on the sea
and the first star is dying quietly.
Here on the sand your driftwood fire has died,
and the charred sticks have spluttered in the tide.
The green waves breathe their monotonous breath,
they make a stony music of their death
foaming and fawning on the pebble shore.
There is no sound of voices any more.
The waves break, break, in their cold miseries,
they will not leave their last lamenting kiss,
suck soul from stones and vapour it away,
which groaning they return, sighing repay.
Sleep Alasdair, cold ash by the cold sea,
and be as cold as sea or stone can be:
until from this bare green and crested white
the wasted ash of men shall rise in light.